John Paul II Visits Rural America

Editor: Jean LemMon
Executive Editor: Doug Holthaus
Art Director: Roger Ihlenfeldt
Senior Graphic Designer: Deetra Leech
Publisher: Del Rusher
Contributing Photographers: Linda Bender, Father John Buscemi, Sister Jean Byrne, Bill Connell, Peter Dubec, Mimi Dunlap, David Finch, George Fletcher, Bob Hawks, Lawrence Helton, Doug Holthaus, Thomas Hooper, Michael Jensen, Bob Kelly, Deetra Leech, Nick Merrick, Bob Nandell, Iowa Governor Robert D. Ray, D. C. Riggott, Ralph Sanders, Perry Struse, Ozzie Sweet, Steve Umhoefer

Pilgrimage

Come, let us go up to the mountain of the Lord,
to the house of the God of Jacob;
that he may teach us his ways
and that we may walk in his paths.

—Isaiah 2:3

Throughout the centuries, Christians have made pilgrimages—enduring hardships and sacrificing material gains and physical comforts—to satisfy a deep spiritual need and to answer a special calling. 340,000 pilgrims felt a similar calling as they traveled from every corner of the nation to join the throng at Des Moines' Living History Farms.

Still more pilgrims flocked to the Des Moines Municipal Airport. And, at St. Patrick's of Irish Settlement, a cluster of parishioners made their way to the small, white frame church. For them, the way of the pilgrimage was a path traveled every Sunday. But on this occasion, the spirit was different. They, too, were pilgrims about to meet a pilgrim pope.

Soon, Pope John Paul II would stand on American soil, look out over America's fertile farmlands and create in each of us a newly awakened sense of responsibility—for the land and for each other. This is the true spirit of a pilgrimage—the feeling of being drawn together in a bond of love, concern, rededication and renewal. And it was to experience this—the spirit of the pilgrimage—that people of all ages and all faiths journeyed to the center of America's heartland to welcome Pope John Paul II.

Hawks

Merrick

Photo, preceding page: Sanders

4

Dunlap

*Then I will go to the altar of God,
to God my exceeding joy . . .*
                              —Psalm 43:4

Bender

Hawks   Finch

Why Iowa?

The fields are garmented with flocks and the valleys blanketed with grain. They shout and sing for joy.

—Psalm 65:14

Why would a pope visit Iowa? As a state it is relatively sparse in population, largely rural—and, for the most part, non-Catholic.

As a symbol of America's farming, however, Iowa is a perfectly natural choice for a papal visit. Situated in the center of America's agricultural "heartland" states, Iowa encompasses some of the richest, most productive land on earth. Both large and small family farms are found in the Hawkeye state.

A second, very sound and very human reason for Pope John Paul II to visit Iowa was—he had been invited!

A simple, straight-from-the-heart letter was sent to the Holy Father by Joseph A. Hays, a Truro, Iowa, farmer. He believed it perfectly plausible that Pope John Paul II would accept his invitation. After all, John Paul II was a pope concerned with land use and food production—concerns also shared by the National Catholic Rural Life Conference, headquartered in Des Moines.

This was a pope who has created world-wide awareness that the land is a precious gift from God and should be used wisely. Farmers in America's heartland realize that fact as keenly as anyone anywhere in the world.

And, finally, this was a pope concerned with farmers—the people who are dependent on the land for their livelihoods. He has made it a point to visit rural people on his travels in Mexico and in his native Poland. Therefore, it was not impossible to believe that Pope John Paul II might also visit some portion of Rural America. And in that case—why *not* Iowa?

Photo, preceding page: Sanders

Kruse

19 · July · 1979

To His Holiness Pope John Paul II

We here at St. Marys, Iowa were delighted to hear of your reported visit to the Midwest. Possibly one of the most young and enthusiastic groups of Representatives in the Church in America today is our own rural life People. The Title of our program is "Strangers and Guests Toward Community in the Heartland" with a grass roots study on land. The Study originates from the Bishops of regions seven, eight and nine. We here are especially pleased to have a real rural Bishop, our own Maurice J. Dingman of the Diocese of Des Moines. our Regional director is Msgr Paul Connelly from here at St. Marys, Iowa.

Our Prayer here in the Heartland of our United States is that more People become aware of our program, develope a true concern for our land and its use by Mankind. In this way we can be a stepping stone in the Proper use of our land for the betterment of Mankind. Also it is our request and desire to share company with one, if not the most humane Pope of the Church, Pope John Paul II. In the event that you are to be in the area as reported in October of this year we would very much appriciate an audience with you. Please give firm consideration to our Plea and Pray for us in our Cause.

Yours in Hope and Prayers

Joseph A. Hays

JOSEPH A. HAYS
RT. 1 TRURO IOWA 50257

Struse

Joseph A. Hays with his wife, Ann, and their children Paul, 17, Mark, 15, Theresa, 13, and Ronda, 11.

In an outdoor press conference held August 29, 1979, Maurice J. Dingman, Bishop of the Catholic Diocese of Southwest Iowa (Des Moines), announced that the Holy Father, Pope John Paul II, would visit the Living History Farms near Des Moines on Thursday, October 4, 1979.

"I express a deep sense of gratitude to the Holy Father for accepting the invitation to honor the diocese, the local community and the State of Iowa as well as the heartland area of America with his presence. It is an unprecedented event in our lives.

"The visit of the Holy Father is a 'moment of grace' for the Church and the community. It is an event whose impact will be experienced for years to come.

"A monumental task awaits us in making the physical preparations. But an even greater task is our spiritual preparation. The event itself will pass. But the fruits of the visit will endure."

Symbol
of Rural America

You care for the earth, give it water,
you fill it with riches.
Your river in heaven brims over
to provide its grain . . .

—Psalm 65:9

It is the dignity of those who work on the land and of all those engaged in different levels of agricultural development which must be unceasingly proclaimed and promoted.

These words, first spoken by Pope Paul VI, echoed across the hillsides of the Living History Farms as the area, a living monument to agriculture, became an outdoor cathedral for the historic visit of Pope John Paul II.

From its inception in 1967, the Living History Farms has celebrated the land as a gift from God, entrusted to those who farm it. Here, on 600 acres of fertile Iowa farmland, visitors can experience our continuing relationship to that gift as they view high-powered diesel equipment working the fields of the Farm of Today and Tomorrow—or see a team of horses performing the same tasks on the 1900 Farm.

The work—and the life-style—of early settlers are captured in the Pioneer Farm of 1845. And the character of a small rural Iowa town of the late 1800s is recreated in Walnut Hill.

At one end of this village stands the original Flynn mansion, as stately as when Martin Flynn, an Irish Catholic immigrant, built it in 1870. At the other end of Walnut Hill rises a gentle knoll topped by a pair of rugged oak trees. It was here the platform for the Holy Father's visit was built. And it is here where an ecumenical Church of the Land will be erected, creating a place where visitors can stop and meditate on the blessings of the land.

The Living History Farms, like Pope John Paul II, is concerned with the stewardship of this land—with the future of agriculture and the future of mankind. The land, is, indeed, God's gift—but it is our responsibility.

Dunlap

Photo, preceding page: Dunlap   **1845 Pioneer Farm**   Dun

Dun

Dun

. . . good stewards of
God's varied grace.
—1 Peter 4:10

1900 Farm

Dun

Dunlap

Dunl

Farm of Today and Tomorrow

Transformation

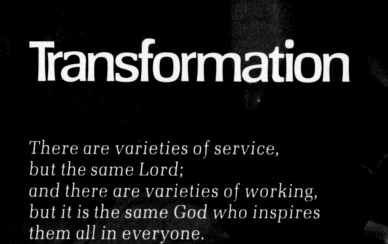

There are varieties of service,
but the same Lord;
and there are varieties of working,
but it is the same God who inspires
them all in everyone.

—1 Corinthians 12:5-6

O n a quiet, tree-lined street in Des Moines resides the Bishop of the Des Moines Diocese. Unlike most residences, however, this one hardly can be termed "private." At all times, Bishop Maurice Dingman's doors are open to meetings, conferences, and retreats as well as being a center of warmth, friendship and fellowship. But with the Pope about to arrive, the "Bishop's house" on 37th Street was being transformed into "headquarters" for the papal visit.

The tree-lined street became a car-lined street. The quiet of this sedate old home was shattered by constantly ringing telephones. Meetings were held around the clock in every possible inch of space, including porches, bedrooms—even the laundry room. Where previous meetings had dealt primarily with church matters, now the subjects under discussion were press credentials, sanitation, transportation, medical facilities and food service. Where religious and laity of the community used to meet, now the meeting rosters included Secret Service, the National Guard, media reporters, photographers, site coordinators and civic officials. The kitchen bustled with women of the community, donating their time and food to nourish the non-stop workers. And in the tiny, second floor chapel, a prayer vigil was kept for the success of the Pope's Pilgrimage to Rural America.

Yet, despite the flurry of activity preceding the arrival of Pope John Paul II, the Bishop's house never stopped being a friendly, hospitable place—a place of welcome, of enthusiasm, of caring, of dedication, of prayer.

Photo, preceding page: Struse

Even the gently rolling hills of the Living History Farms were to undergo a transformation for the Holy Father's visit. Here, rising out of a grassy knoll, a natural outdoor cathedral emerged—designed to be part of the land, laden with gifts of the harvest and adorned with specially crafted pieces of art to be used in worship, created by local artisans.

The focal point of the natural "cathedral" was an asymmetrical 40x80-foot platform, designed to suit the land and the liturgy—not to conform to preconceived ideas about cathedral space. The materials selected for the canopied platform also echoed this "liturgy-of-the-land." Rough-sawn boards edged the stairs and terraced the platform. Carpeting was chosen for its warm earth-brown color and distinctly corded surface, meant to symbolize plowed fields. And topping one end of this unique platform, a lofty metal framework stretched skyward, waiting to display the huge quilted banner—the design symbol of Pope John Paul II's visit to Rural America.

Access roads had to be built. Trees needed to be shaped to improve the view. Hundreds of metal barrels had to be trucked in and arranged for crowd control. High-rising platforms were needed for sound equipment and media photographers.

Architects, heavy equipment operators, carpenters, metalworkers, landscape specialists, floral artists—all worked with a genuine sense of dedication. The transformation of the Living History Farms' fields was a story of unparalleled cooperation—and these people were making it happen. This was, indeed, a cathedral!

Dun

Jens

sen

nlap

nlap

Whatever you do . . .
do it in the name of the
Lord Jesus . . .
— Colossians 3:17

Jen

Jensen

Dun

Jens

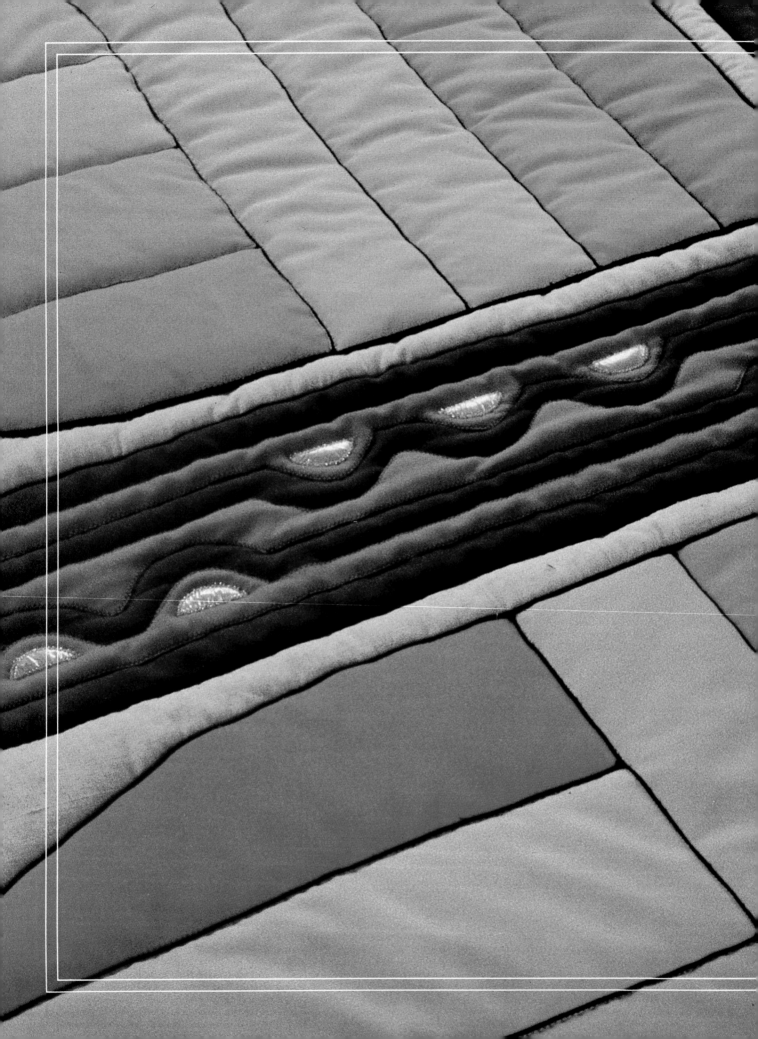

Art offerings

Blessed are you, Lord, God of all creation.
Through your goodness
we have . . . [these gifts] . . . to offer
which earth has given
and human hands have made.
—Liturgy of the Eucharist, The Roman Missal

Praise God in his sanctuary. Praise him in his mighty firmament (Psalm 150:1). Praise him with works of art!

The celebration symbol of Pope John Paul II's visit to Rural America was created to praise God in both his sanctuary and his mighty firmament. The symbol, executed as a huge quilted banner, was hung at one end of the platform constructed in the cathedral space of the Living History Farms.

This colorful design, created by Father John Buscemi of the Diocese of Madison, Wisconsin, is a visual interpretation of the First Reading of the Mass, Galatians 6:14. *May I never boast of anything but the cross of our Lord Jesus Christ. . . . All that really matters is that we are created anew.*

Father Buscemi centered his design on a cross, accented by shapes that symbolize furrowed soil and seeds. This cross reminds us that the Word of God can take root only in lives prepared to receive it.

Four "fields" are secured within the arms of the cross. Their shapes represent the contours of plowed land. And their colors take us through the four seasons, reminding us that the blessing of harvest can only be achieved when the earth and the seed move through the full cycle of time.

To translate this design symbol into the magnificent banner used in the celebration, a talented group of quilters from Cross Plains, Lodi, Waunakee and Madison, Wisconsin, worked with dedication—and precision. It was in their hands that this offering of beauty and scriptural significance took form and became reality.

Photo, preceding page: Jensen

Umhoefe

Inset photo: Umhoefer

Umhoefe

Jen

 Praise him with trumpet sound (Psalm 150:3)—and with the sound of power saws and hammers—and with the sound of hands rubbing oil into a mirror-smooth wooden surface.

The altar, lectern and chair, like the entire outdoor cathedral environment, were designed by Father Buscemi and were created as acts of praise by local artisans using their God-given talents.

Each art offering has special significance and symbolism that makes it appropriate for a celebration of the land. And each was planned to augment the outdoor cathedral's aura of noble simplicity—to contribute to the quiet beauty of autumn in Rural America.

The altar, designed with a convoluted front to symbolize plowed fields, was crafted of 100-year-old white oak timbers salvaged from an Iowa corn crib. It, as well as the lectern and chair, were projects worked on by the entire staff of Des Moines Millwork Manufacturing, Inc., and Breiholz Construction Company. The exquisite finishing of the wood pieces was one example of the praise gifts of time and energy offered by the many skilled craftspersons from the Des Moines area.

In the same way artists sign their prize canvasses, all the craftsmen who worked on the altar carved their names into the bottom of it. For them, building the altar was not just a job, it was creating a work of art—a work of praise—in wood.

Inset photo: Jensen

Jens

Jens

 Praise him with lute and harp (Psalm 150:3)—and with a silver needle dancing in and out through natural-colored homespun fabric.

Diane Mohrfeld's offering of praise was the needle-art rendering of the celebration symbol on the cover of the Book of the Gospel. Diane, an art and photography instructor at Dowling High School in West Des Moines, stitched the multi-colored symbol in the center of the cover. And at the bottom edge of the book, the symbol's furrowed field and seed design stretched across the fabric like acres of fertile farmland. A similar book, incorporating the field and seed design and used by the Holy Father, was stitched by Peg Haller.

Rural America Welcom
Pope John Paul II
Feast of St. Francis of As
October 4, 1979

e Order for the Eucharistic Celeb

Introductory Rites

Jen

nders

Praise him with timbrel and dance (Psalm 150:4)—and a shuttle of wool skipping through the warp of a loom.

The altar cloth was a gift of praise created by Connie Forneris, a weaving instructor at the Des Moines Art Center.

In her skilled hands, the design symbol of the papal visit emerged in a subtle natural coloration, woven into the 40 x 50-inch cloth used to cover the altar.

God's gifts of material—the wool of sheep that graze on the land—had been returned to serve in worshipping Him. God's gift of talent also had been used in praise of Him.

nsen

Praise him with strings and pipe (Psalm 150:4)—and with clay whirling and spinning on a potter's wheel.

James C. Ross, a pottery instructor at Dowling High School in West Des Moines, created his offerings of praise in ceramics. It was Jim's hands that shaped the chalice, the plate and the bowl holding the wine decanter used during the liturgy.

The beautifully crafted contemporary vessels which held the bread and wine were, indeed, gifts with which to praise the Lord—and the earth—from which the pottery had been created.

Jens

Inset photos: Jensen

Jens

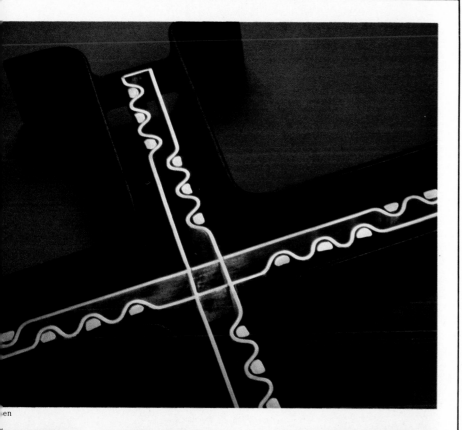

en

en

 Praise him with sounding cymbals (Psalm 150:5)—and with hammering metal and the sparks of a welding torch.

Metalworker Charles Punelli devoted nearly 100 hours to creating the processional cross used in the celebration. Its design is an adaptation of the celebration symbol, wrought in various metals, including brass and copper.

During the liturgy, the cross, designed by Father Buscemi, rose above the offering gifts on the platform—calling attention to the fact that there are a multitude of ways to praise God—many of them through creative art forms.

Let everything that breathes praise the Lord!

—Psalm 150:6

WORLD REPORT

SALT or NATO 'crisis'

POPE BRINGS HIS HISTO
JOURNEY TO IOWA TOD

merce
ary
quits

a Wire Services
.C. — Juanita
's first female
merce, submitted
resignation to
ident Carter
nesday, she said.
reps cited
rsonal family
ns" for leaving
Cabinet job,
ording to
mmerce
esman Ernest
n, who added
feels she has
away from her
ee years and at
ith them."

White House
e today that
the resignation

uke Chancellor
at Kreps would
ty Nov. 1. She
m her job as a
esident and

ously consider-
am since late
nband's health
who asked for

husband, Dr.
Jr. fired
to his mouth,
ness professor
orth Carolina,
the day from
North Carolina

reps now was

D.M.
FOR
SAYS

Bishop
to pa

October 4,1979

This is the day which the Lord has made;
let us rejoice and be glad in it.

—Psalm 118:24

Waiting

Merrick

Long before sunrise, early morning pilgrims braved a chilly, penetrating wind to stake out their waiting places—on the grassy slopes, along fences, huddled together for warmth and conversation. The waiting began—at both the airport and the Living History Farms.

Diversions were created. Card games flourished. Reading was a favorite time-passer, as was getting acquainted with fellow pilgrims. Lunches were eaten—as much for something to do as for the nourishment they provided. Children—and adults—caught catnaps in strange positions in strange places. And still the waiting went on.

Throughout the morning, the waiting at the Living History Farms was punctuated with songs of praise offered by high school and college choirs.

At midday, the sun scuttled in and out among threatening clouds. The wind blew in gusts and rustled in whispers. The waiting became more prayerful. An ecumenical prayer service caught up the cold, tired pilgrims and directed their thoughts away from the long hours that had preceded this moment. The spirit of the day spread through the crowd.

Pilgrims were no longer sitting on blankets in the fields like impatient summer picnickers—they were worshippers in the Lord's Holy Temple.

The waiting was over.

Photo, preceding page: Fletcher

Mer

rick

Merrick

tcher

. . .with great compassion I will gather you.
—Isaiah 54:7

Hoo

Le

oper

ech

Welcome

Mer

The red carpet was ready. State and local dignitaries were in their places. Little Tommy Anania, chosen from among parochial school students of the Des Moines Diocese to greet the Holy Father, exhibited a typical nine-year-old's nervousness as he stood with his armful of flowers. Shepherd I glided effortlessly into position. The time was 1:47 p.m.

A numbed-from-the-cold crowd suddenly came alive—cheering, shouting, waving banners. The famous figure emerged from the papal-crested 727. Pope John Paul II was in Iowa!

Here was the first pope ever to visit the Midwest—only the second pope to visit the United States. From the moment the Holy Father stepped off the plane, he and the crowd were one in spirit. The friendliness, the humanness of this leader of the Church transcended all differences of age, religious faith or social status.

Official greetings were exchanged, gifts were presented, formalities were executed. And then, the Holy Father, in a gesture characteristic of this unique man, spontaneously moved toward the crowd where he talked with elderly and handicapped persons, patted youngsters, and grasped the outstretched hands. His presence was felt—even by those who were not close enough to touch him. But he touched *them*—with a warm smile, with a hand raised in blessing—with a real sense that this was the Vicar of Christ, come at last to visit the people of Rural America.

Mer

Mer

44

errick

Mer

*Give him a most hearty welcome,
in the Lord . . .*

—Philippians 2:29

Rig

bec

rrick

Prelude

*. . . the messenger of the covenant
in whom you delight, behold,
he is coming . . .*

—Malachi 3:1

As the sun eased its way up over the hills of the Living History Farms, steady streams of pilgrims moved over the contours of the land. The day, like a musical prelude, started slowly, building in intensity as the morning passed.

And while people on the hillsides patiently waited out the hours until the arrival of the Holy Father, a whole symphony of behind-the-scenes specialists started their countdown.

Construction workers, rivaling circus performers in high-wire artistry, lashed down the canopy over the papal chair. Another team of workers battled a brisk wind to hang the 10x10-foot quilted banner, focal point of the cathedral platform. Soundmen fine-tuned their equipment, while photographers, perching high on camera stands, checked out their photo angles—and florists gave the colorful array of autumn-hued flowers a last minute watering. Various choral groups offered their praise through song, and an ecumenical service underscored the unity of the crowd.

Then, with only minutes to wait until the Holy Father's arrival, a special group of communicants, including representatives of Native Americans and Indo-Chinese refugees, filed into the platform area to be seated. They were quickly joined by 10 persons representing the National Catholic Rural Life Conference from across the U.S. The two hundred and fifty Iowa priests and deacons who would distribute communion took their places beside the platform. A restlessness rippled through the crowd. Everything was ready.

Then, like the roll of a tympani, the whir of helicopter rotors overhead brought the prelude to a triumphant conclusion. The celebration was about to begin.

Photo, preceding page: Holthaus

50

nders

unlap

Leech

Come; for all is now ready.
—Luke 14:17

Holth

Le

ers

Celebration

Let the heavens be glad
and the earth rejoice;
Let the sea and
what fills it resound;
Let the plains be joyful
and all that is in them . . .
—Psalm 96:11-12

Eucharistic Celebration
Feast of St. Francis of Assisi

Hooper

Dubec

"All creatures of our God and King,
Lift up your voice and with us sing
Alleluia! Alleluia!"
　　—All Creatures of our God and King
　　by William H. Draper, (Based on
　　St. Francis of Assisi's
　　"Canticle of Creation").

"On this feast of St. Francis we pray
with the liturgy that the Father
may help us 'to reflect the image of
Christ through a life of poverty and
humility—by walking in the footsteps
of Francis of Assisi and by imitating
his joyful love.'
　　"To a pilgrim pope, we a
pilgrim people extend our heartfelt
welcome!"
　　—Address of welcome given by
　　　the Most Rev. Maurice J. Dingman,
　　　Bishop of Des Moines

Dubec

First reading

"May I never boast of anything but the cross of our Lord Jesus Christ! Through it, the world has been crucified to me and I to the world. It means nothing whether one is circumcised or not. All that matters is that one is created anew. Peace and mercy on all who follow this rule of life, and on the Israel of God.

"Henceforth, let no man trouble me, for I bear the brand marks of Jesus in my body.

"Brothers, may the favor of our Lord Jesus Christ be with your spirit. Amen."

—Galatians 6:14-18

Fi

Byrne

Gospel

"On one occasion Jesus said: 'Father, Lord of heaven and earth, to you I offer praise; for what you have hidden from the learned and the clever you have revealed to the merest children.' Father, it is true. You have graciously willed it so. Everything has been given over to me by my Father. No one knows the Son but the Father, and no one knows the Father but the Son—and anyone to whom the Son wishes to reveal him.

" 'Come to me, all you who are weary and find life burdensome, and I will refresh you. Take my yoke upon your shoulders and learn from me, for my yoke is easy and my burden is light.' "

—Matthew 11:25-30

ndell

Buscemi

Hooper

The Homily of Pope John Paul II

Dear brothers and sisters in Christ:
Here in the heartland of America, in the middle of the bountiful fields at harvest time, I come to celebrate the Eucharist. As I stand in your presence in this period of autumn harvest, those words which are repeated whenever people gather for the Eucharist seem to be so appropriate: "Blessed are you, Lord God of all creation, through your goodness we have this bread to offer which earth has given and human hands have made."

As one who has always been close to nature, let me speak to you today about the land, the earth, and that "which earth has given and human hands have made."

The land is God's gift entrusted to people from the very beginning. It is God's gift, given by a loving Creator as a means of sustaining the life which he had created. But the land is not only God's gift; it is also man's responsibility. Man, himself created from the dust of the earth (Genesis 3:7), was made its master (Genesis 1:26). In order to bring forth fruit, the land would depend upon the genius and skillfulness, the sweat and the toil of the people to whom God would entrust it. Thus the food which would sustain life on earth is willed by God to be both that "which earth has given and human hands have made."

To all of you who are farmers and all who are associated with agricultural production I want to say this: The Church highly esteems your work. Christ himself showed his esteem for agricultural life when he

described God his Father as "the vinedresser" (John 15:1). You cooperate with the Creator, the "vinedresser," in sustaining and nurturing life. You fulfill the command of God given at the very beginning: "Fill the earth and subdue it" (Genesis 1:28). Here in the heartland of America, the valleys and hills have been blanketed with grain, the herds and the flocks have multiplied many times over. By hard work you have become masters of the earth and you have subdued it. By reason of the abundant fruitfulness which modern agricultural advances have made possible, you support the lives of millions who themselves do not work on the land, but who live because of what you produce. Mindful of this, I make my own the words of my beloved predecessor Paul VI: "It is the dignity of those who work on the land and of all those engaged in different levels of research and action in the field of agricultural development which must be unceasingly proclaimed and promoted." (Address to the World Food Conference, November 9, 1974, no. 4.)

What then are the attitudes that should pervade man's relationship to the land? As always we must look for the answer beginning with Jesus, for, as Saint Paul says: "In your minds you must be the same as Christ Jesus" (Philippians 2:5). In the life of Jesus, we see a real closeness to the land. In his teaching, he referred to the "birds of the air" (Matthew 6:26), the "lilies of the field" (Matthew 7:17). He talked about the farmer who went out to sow the seed (Matthew 13:4 ff); and he referred to his heavenly father as the "vinedresser" (John 15:1), and to himself as the "good shepherd" (John 10:14).

This closeness to nature, this spontaneous awareness of creation as a gift from God, as well as the blessing of a close-knit family—characteristics of farm life in every age including our own—these were part of the life of Jesus. Therefore I invite you to let your attitudes always be the same as those of Christ Jesus.

Three attitudes in particular are appropriate for rural life. In the first place: gratitude. Recall the first words of Jesus in the Gospel we have just heard, words of gratitude to his heavenly father: "Father, Lord of heaven and earth, to you I offer praise." Let this be your attitude as well. Every day the farmer is reminded of how much he depends upon God. From the heavens come the rain, the wind and the sunshine. They occur without the farmer's command or control. The farmer prepares the soil, plants the seed, and cultivates the crop. But God makes it grow; he alone is the source of life. Even the natural disasters, such as hailstorms and drought, tornadoes or floods, remind the farmer of his dependence upon God. Surely it was this awareness that prompted the early pilgrims to America to establish the feast which you call "Thanksgiving." After every harvest, whatever it may have been that year, with humility and thankfulness the farmer makes his own the prayer of Jesus: "Father, Lord of heaven and earth, to you I offer praise."

Secondly, the land must be conserved with care since it is intended to be fruitful for generation upon generation. You who live in the heartland of America have been entrusted with some of the earth's best land: the soil so rich in minerals, the climate so favorable for producing bountiful crops, with fresh water and unpolluted air available all around you. You are stewards of some of the most important resources God has given to the world. Therefore conserve the land well, so that your children's children and generations after them will inherit an even richer land than was entrusted to you. But also remember what the heart of your vocation is. While it is true here that farming today provides an economic livelihood for the farmer, still it will always be more than an enterprise of profit-making. In farming, you cooperate with the Creator in the very sustenance of life on earth.

In the third place, I want to speak about generosity, a generosity which arises from the fact that "God destined the earth and all it contains for all men and all peoples so that all created things would be shared fairly by all mankind under the guidance of justice tempered by charity" (*Guadium et Spes*, 69). You who are farmers today are stewards of a gift from God which was intended for the good of all humanity. You have the potential to provide food for the millions who have nothing to eat and thus to help rid the world of famine. To you I direct the same question asked by Paul VI five years ago: . . . if the potential of nature is immense, if that of the mastery of the human genius over the universe seems almost unlimited, what is it that is too often missing . . . except that generosity, that anxiety which is stimulated by the sight of the sufferings and the miseries of the poor, that deep conviction that the whole family suffers when one of its members is in distress? (Address to the World Food Conference, November 9, 1974, no. 9.)

Recall the time when Jesus saw the hungry crowd gathered on the hillside. What was his response? He did not content himself with expressing his compassion. He gave his disciples the command: "Give them something to eat yourselves" (Matthew 14:16). Did he not intend those same words for us today, for us who live at the closing of the twentieth century, for us who have the means available to feed the hungry of the world? Let us respond generously to his command by sharing the fruit of our labor, by contributing to others the knowledge we have gained, by being the promoters of rural development everywhere and by defending the right to work of the rural population, since every person has a right to useful employment.

Farmers everywhere provide bread for all humanity, but it is Christ alone who is the bread of life. He alone satisfies the deepest hunger of humanity. As Saint Augustine said: "Our hearts are restless until they rest in you" (*Confessions I*, 1). While we are mindful of the physical hunger of millions of our brothers and sisters on all continents, at this Eucharist we are reminded that the deepest hunger lies in the human soul. To all who acknowledge this hunger within them Jesus says: "Come to me, all you who are weary and find life burdensome, and I will refresh you." My brothers and sisters in Christ: Let us listen to these words with all our heart. They are directed to everyone of us. To all who till the soil, to all who benefit from the fruit of their labors, to every man and woman on earth, Jesus says: "Come to me . . . and I will refresh you." Even if all the physical hunger of the world were

satisfied, even if everyone who is hungry were fed by his or her own labor or by the generosity of others, the deepest hunger of man would still exist.

We are reminded in the letter of Saint Paul to the Galatians: "All that matters is that one is created anew." Only Christ can create one anew; and this new creation finds its beginning only in his Cross and Resurrection. In Christ alone all creation is restored to its proper order. Therefore, I say: Come, all of you, to Christ. He is the bread of life. Come to Christ and you will never be hungry again.

Bring with you to Christ the products of your hands, the fruit of the land, that "which earth has given and human hands have made." At this altar these gifts will be transformed into the Eucharist of the Lord.

Bring with you your efforts to make fruitful the land, your labor and your weariness. At this altar, because of the life, death and Resurrection of Christ, all human activity is sanctified, lifted up and fulfilled.

Bring with you the poor, the sick, the exiled and the hungry; bring all who are weary and find life burdensome. At this altar they will be refreshed, for his yoke is easy and his burden light.

Above all, bring your families and dedicate them anew to Christ, so that they may continue to be the working, living and loving community where nature is revered, where burdens are shared and where the Lord is praised in gratitude.

The preceding is the prepared text of Pope John Paul II's homily delivered at the Living History Farms, October 4, 1979.

Sanders

"For people who live on and in the land—for American Indians, farm workers, coal miners, timber workers, share croppers, family farmers and ranchers—that the dignity of their call to steward the land will be recognized, and that they will be justly rewarded for their labor and for what they produce,
    Let us pray to the Lord."
                —General Intercessions

K

Le

ks

lers

Sanders

h

Sanders

Ho

D

nell

y

Dub

"One bread, one body,
one Lord of all,
one cup of blessing which we bless.
And we, though many,
throughout the earth,
we are one body in this one Lord."
— *One Bread, One Body*
by John Foley, S.J.

wks

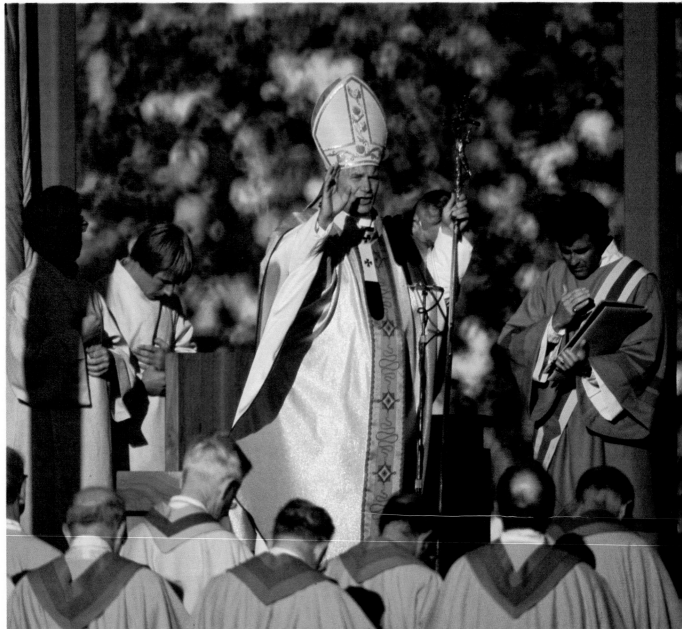

Sanders

Sanders

"O beautiful for spacious skies
For amber waves of grain,
For purple mountain majesties
Above the fruited plain.
America! America!
God shed his grace on thee,
And crown thy good with brotherhood
From sea to shining sea."
—*America the Beautiful*
by Katherine Lee Bates

The shepherd

Jesus said to Simon Peter—
"Simon, son of John, do you love me?"
"Yes, Lord," he answered, "you know that I love you."
Jesus said to him, "Take care of my sheep."

—John 21:15

L.

The gnarled silver crosier, carried by the Bishop of Rome, is symbolic of his role as shepherd of the world's 700 million Catholics. With Pope John Paul II, however, the crosier is more than symbolic. In his hands, the staff becomes totally functional—an integral part of him—strong, supportive, guiding. The crosier actually serves as an extenson of the Holy Father's being as he lifts it high above the crowd in a papal blessing that's unique to him.

And seeing this sturdy, robust man striding across the open patches of grass, staff in hand, it's not difficult to visualize him as a true shepherd. Mingling with the crowd—exchanging glances, smiles, friendly words—the strength of this man, this shepherd, becomes apparent. The large, strong hands could easily be the hands of a herdsman—or a farmer. The weather-worn face, with its magnificent character, might well be that of a man who tilled the soil. And when he speaks, his words ring with authenticity. He speaks the language of the land.

"The land must be conserved with care since it is intended to be fruitful for generation upon generation."

Listeners, silent and attentive, grasped his message with a feeling these were not merely words read from a script. They came from the heart of a man who knows the land, knows his flock and their needs and, like a shepherd, cares about them—not just at this time and in this place, but for generation upon generation.

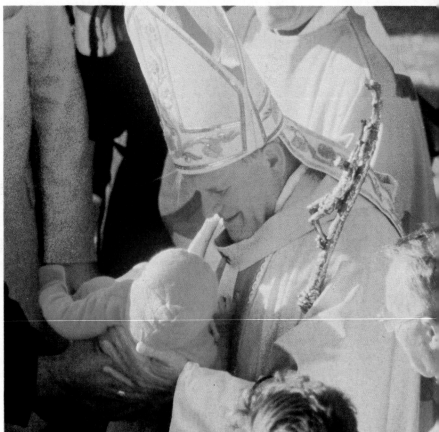

Photo, preceding page: Buscemi

Ho.

oper

wks

Hawks

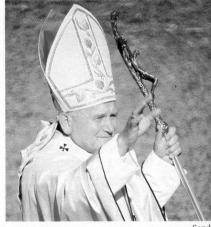

. . . *You shall be shepherd of my people* . . .
—2 Samuel 5:2

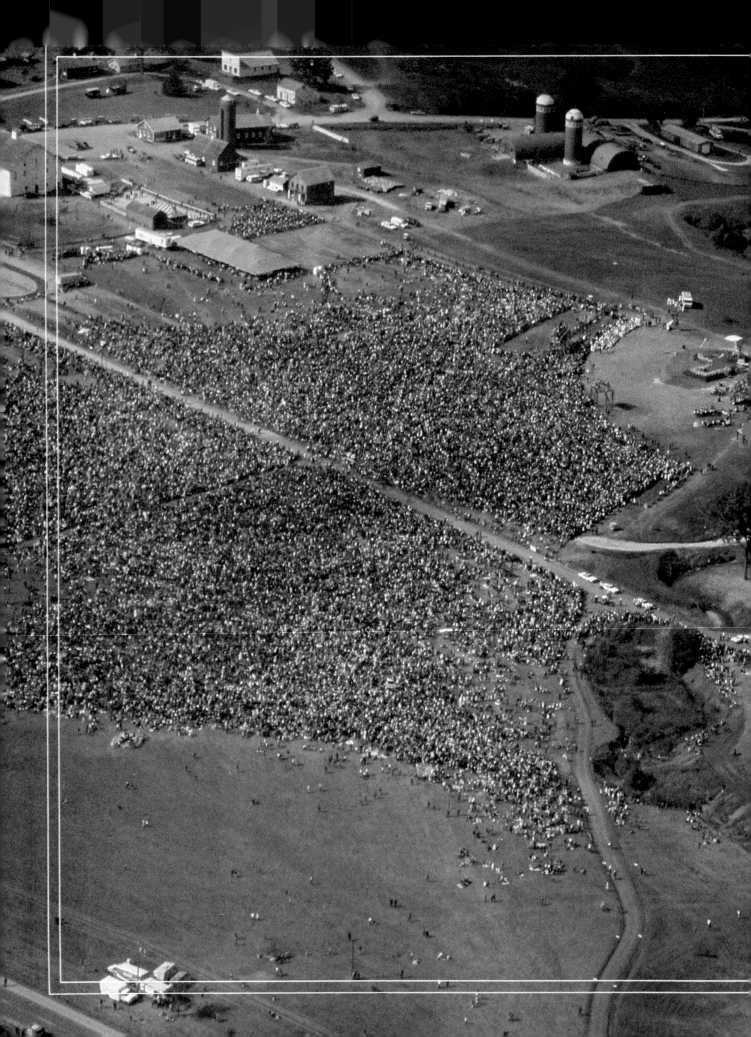

Pilgrims

There does not exist
among you Jew or Greek,
slave or freeman, male or female.
All are one in Christ Jesus.

—Galatians 3:28

A pilgrimage, like an intricate
tapestry, is made up of many
different elements, all woven
together to produce a single,
beautiful design.

In the tapestry of humanity
gathered at the Living History Farms,
elements varied from members of
ethnic groups in colorful native
costume to banner-carrying groups
expressing a variety of sentiments.
There were people of all ages, all
races, in all manners of dress—a
dazzling kaleidoscope of pilgrims.
But all had the same purpose—to
see, hear and be touched by the
Holy Father.

Each of these pilgrims had come
to this place with his or her unique
set of characteristics, created by a
town, a neighborhood, a family, a
job, a circle of friends. Yet, each
individual was woven into the
tapestry until the vast sea of people
was no longer 340,000 individuals.
The pilgrims were not Iowans and
non-Iowans—not Catholics and non-
Catholics—not young or old—strong
or handicapped. This was a single
entity, born of a common spirit. This
was the living church.

*So we, though many, are one
body in Christ, and individually
members one of another.*
— Romans 12:5

Dur

Photo, preceding page: Governor Robert D. Ray, Iowa   Holth

Merr

er

h

And the Lord said,
"Behold, they are one
people..."

—Genesis 11:6

ly

St. Patrick's
of Irish Settlement

*. . . I hope to visit you and talk to you personally,
so that our joy may be complete.*

—2 John 12

Away from the crush of the cities, the traffic, and the noise, Pope John Paul II spent three-quarters of an hour in the quiet of a small, rural parish, touching—and being touched—by the families who are St. Patrick's of Irish Settlement.

It was here, with the people who live on—and by—the land, that the Holy Father seemed most comfortable. Here, in this 127-year-old parish, he spoke eloquently of the privilege of worshipping together in this setting. He spoke of the farmers' closeness to nature and the "human dimension" of a small community. And the parishioners listened with rapt attention.

This was the Holy Father, the Bishop of Rome. This was the day each of the 204 members of St. Patrick's had waited for. And yet, in the presence of this gentle, loving man, the awe of the occasion was leavened by a comfortable feeling of familiarity. Children squirmed in their pews just as they do during a regular Sunday Mass. Before the Holy Father's arrival, the servers, robed in their white albs, played Frisbee on the lawn while ladies of the church organized food for the parish potluck later that afternoon.

This was the real St. Patrick's—the unpretentious, spirit-filled body of worshippers chosen to represent all the small, rural churches of America. This was the "human dimension" of which the Holy Father spoke when he told the parish "a community with a human face must also reflect the face of Christ."

Photo, preceding page: Struse

ton

Pope John Paul II's Message to St. Patrick's

Struse

Dear brothers and sisters:
It gives me great pleasure to be here today with you, in the heartland of America, in this lovely Saint Patrick's Church at the Irish Settlement. My pastoral journey through the United States would have seemed incomplete without a visit, although short, to a rural community like this. Let me share with you some thoughts that this particular setting brings to mind; and that are prompted by my meeting with the families who make up this rural parish.

To proclaim Jesus Christ and his Gospel is the fundamental task which the Church has received from her Founder, and which she has taken up ever since the dawn of the first Pentecost. The early Christians were faithful to this mission which the Lord Jesus gave them through his Apostles: "They devoted themselves to the apostles' teaching and fellowship, to the breaking of the bread and the prayers" (Acts 2:42). This is what every community of believers must do: proclaim Christ and his Gospel in fellowship and apostolic faith, in prayer and in the celebration of the Eucharist.

How many Catholic parishes have been started like yours in the early beginnings of the settlement of this region: a small, unpretentious church at the center of a group of family farms, a place and a symbol of prayer and fellowship, the heart of a real Christian community where people know each other personally, share each other's problems, and give witness together to the love of Jesus Christ.

On your farms you are close to God's nature; in your work on the land you follow the rhythm of the seasons, and in your hearts you feel close to each other as children of a common Father and as brothers and sisters in Christ. How privileged you are, that in such a setting you can worship God together, celebrate your spiritual unity and help to carry each other's burdens. The 1974 Synod of Bishops in Rome and Paul VI in his Apostolic Exhortation *Evangelii Nuntiandi* have devoted considerable attention to the small communities where a more human dimension is achieved than is possible in a big city or in a sprawling metropolis. Let your small community be a true place of Christian living and of evangelization, not isolating yourselves from the diocese or from the universal Church, knowing that a community with a human face must also reflect the face of Christ.

Feel grateful to God for the blessings he gives you, not least for the blessing of belonging to this rural parish community. May our heavenly Father bless you, each and every one of you. May the simplicity of your life-style and the closeness of your community be the fertile ground for a growing commitment to Jesus Christ, Son of God and Savior of the world.

I for my part thank the Lord for the opportunity he gave me to come and visit you, and as Vicar of Christ to represent him in your midst. Thank you also for your warm welcome and for offering me your hospitality as I prepare for my encounter with the larger group of people at the Living History Farms.

My gratitude goes in a special way to the Bishop of Des Moines for his most cordial invitation. He pointed out many reasons why a visit to Des Moines would be so meaningful: a city that is one of the major agricultural centers of this country; the headquarters also of the dynamic and deserving Catholic Rural Life Conference, whose history is so closely linked to the name of a pastor and a friend of the rural people, Monsignor Luigi Ligutti; a region distinguished by community involvement and family-centered activity; a diocese that is involved, together with all the Catholic bishops of the heartland, in a major effort to build community.

My greetings and best wishes go also to the whole State of Iowa, to the civil authorities and to all the people, who have so generously extended to me a hospitality marked by kindness.

May God bless you through the intercession of Mary, the Mother of Jesus and the Mother of his Church.

The preceding is the prepared text of the Pope's message delivered at St. Patrick's Church of the Irish Settlement near Cumming, Iowa.

*. . . I was a stranger
and you welcomed me.*
—Matthew 25:35

se

ec

Farewell

. . . and this is only the beginning
of what they will do . . .
—Genesis 11:6

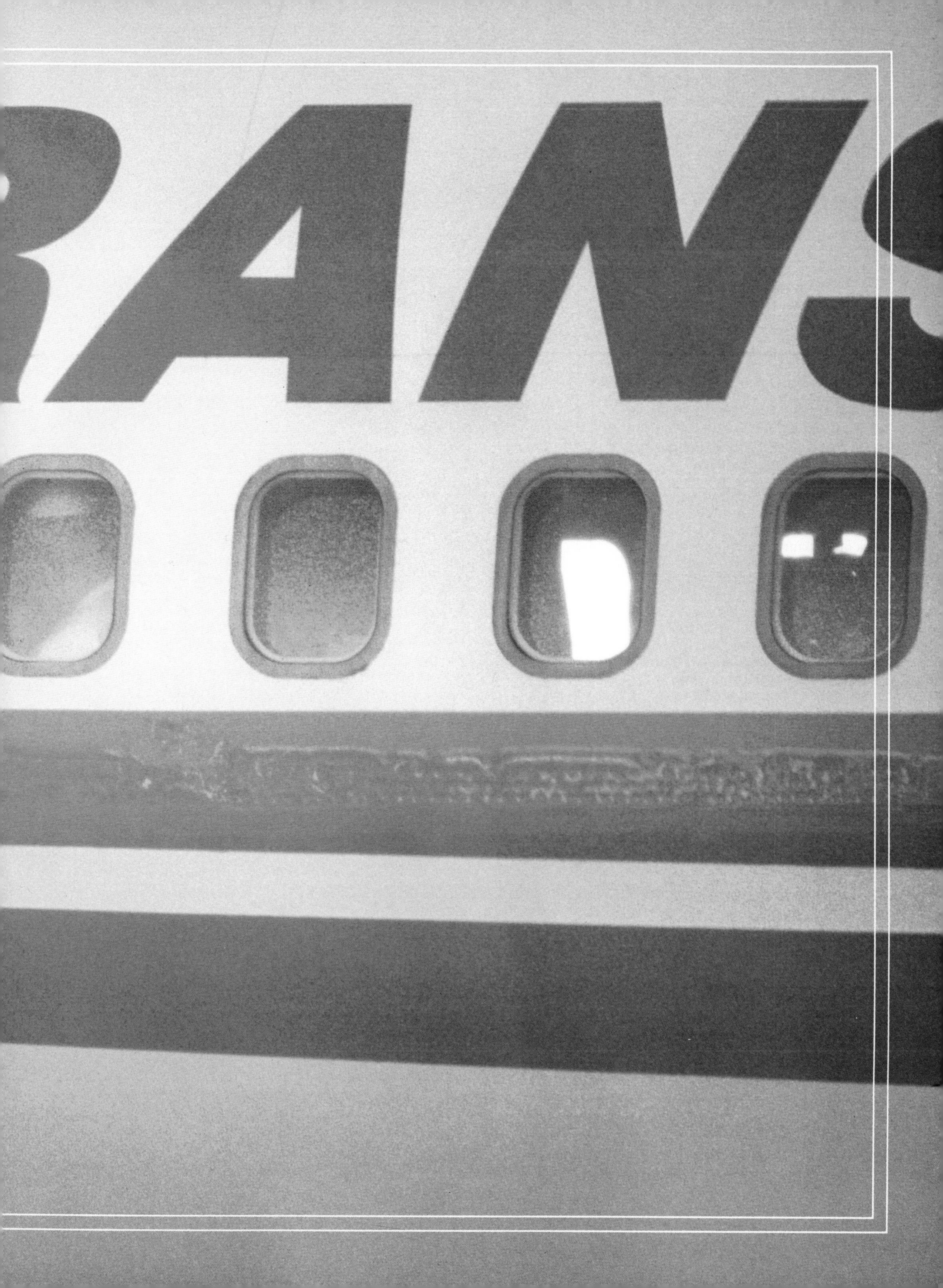
RANS

The visit ends (as all things must), but the experience, the memories of the day, the feelings of goodwill—these things will leave their impressions on us forever.

For a short span of time we forgot our differences and celebrated our similarities. We took stock of the kind of people we are and the blessings that are ours, living in this fertile agricultural area. We lifted our voices and our hearts in praise and gratitude.

As the Holy Father spoke to us—moved through the crowd—became one of us—we were caught up in his spirit of loving concern for all humanity. We were touched by a man of great strength and, with him, we were able to feel our own strengths—the potentials we all have to care about one another, to share our burdens and, together, to rejoice in our blessings.

These are the seeds that have been planted in each of us. And with proper care, these seeds can produce a bountiful harvest of love and brotherhood.

The pilgrimage is over—but the harvest is yet to come.

Photo, preceding page: Merrick

Mer

ck

Prayer for Peace

Lord, make me an instrument of your peace.
Where there is hatred, let me sow love;
Where there is injury, pardon;
Where there is doubt, faith;
Where there is despair, hope;
Where there is darkness, light;
And where there is sadness, joy.

O Divine Master, grant that I may not
So much seek to be consoled as to console;
To be understood as to understand;
To be loved as to love;
For it is in giving that we receive;
It is in pardoning that we are pardoned;
And it is in dying
That we are born to eternal life.

—St. Francis of Assisi

Merrick

. . . the working, living and loving community where nature is revered, where burdens are shared and where the Lord is praised in gratitude.

—Pope John Paul II
Des Moines, Iowa
October 4, 1979

Leech